Man-yee
and the
New School

Written by Mio Debnam

Illustrated by Wendy Tan Shiau Wei

Collins

Chapter 1

Man-yee stood outside her new school.
She was full of fear.

The new town was small and so was the school.
It wasn't like her old school at all.

When Man-yee walked into the classroom, all the children went quiet.

"I'm Laura, where are you from?" one asked.

"Manchester," said Man-yee.

The teacher came in.

She smiled at Man-yee. "This is Ash Class," she said.
"I'm Mrs Parker. Can you tell us about yourself?"

"My name is Man-yee Chan," said Man-yee. "I was born in Manchester, and ..."

"She's called Man!" Mark yelled.
The children sniggered.

Man-yee felt like crawling away and hiding.

No one had made fun of her name in the past.
Mrs Parker hushed the class.

All day, Man-yee caught sight of people sniggering as she passed.

Chapter 2

By home time, she was in tears.

"Man-yee's a charming name," Mrs Parker said.
"This will pass. They'll soon forget."

"How about a nickname?" said Laura.

"Like what?" Man-yee asked.

"Like ... Amanda?" said Laura.

Man-yee sighed. "I'll think about it ..."

After school, Man-yee went to bed. "I don't feel well," she told Mum.

"It's hard starting a new school," Mum said.
"Have some fun this weekend. You'll soon feel better."

Chapter 3

On Sunday, Man-yee put on her training outfit and did some wushu.

Later, she performed for her dad.

When you were born, Grandma said you'd be good at sports!

"So we called you Man-yee!" said Mum.

"What do you mean?" asked Man-yee.

"Your name means quick and fit," explained Dad.

That night, Man-yee couldn't stop smiling.

The next morning at school, Man-yee asked
Mrs Parker if she could talk to the class.

Man-yee got up but she didn't ask them to call her "Amanda".

"Hello, I'm Man-yee," she said with pride.
"My name means 'quick and fit'."

"I was born in Manchester and I love wushu —
it's like kung fu."

敏 宜

quick　fit

"Cool name, Man-yee!" shouted Mark. "Can you show us some wushu?"

Mrs Parker nodded to Man-yee.

Man-yee inhaled, spun around and did a high kick.

The class gasped and clapped.

"Wow! Can you teach me, Man-yee?" said Laura.

Man-yee smiled and nodded.

She loved her name and her new school too!

Man-yee

31

After reading

Letters and Sounds: Phase 5

Word count: 384

Focus phonemes: /ai/ ay, a-e, ey /ee/ ea /igh/ i-e, i /oa/ o, o-e /oo/ ew, ou, u, oul /ar/ a /ow/ ou /or/ al, our, augh, aw, au

Common exception words: of, to, the, into, by, put, full, are, my, she, we, be, said, have, do, were, when, what, where, school, people, Mrs, was, some, love, one

Curriculum links: Physical education; PSHE

National Curriculum learning objectives: Reading/word reading: read accurately by blending the sounds in words that contain the graphemes taught so far, especially recognising alternative sounds for graphemes; Reading/comprehension (KS2): understand what they read, in books they can read independently, by checking that the text makes sense to them, discussing their understanding and explaining the meaning of words in context; making inferences on the basis of what is being said and done; predicting what might happen on the basis of what has been read so far

Developing fluency

- Take turns to read a page. Check that your child uses different voices for the narrator and the different characters.

Phonic practice

- Focus on the /or/ sound. Turn to page 20 and ask your child to find the two words that contain the /or/ sound and the letters that make the sound. (*called – al*; *your – our*)
- Ask your child to identify and sound out the spelling of /or/ in these words:

  born (*or*)   walked (*al*)   yourself (*our*)   crawling (*aw*)
  caught (*augh*)   Laura (*au*)

Extending vocabulary

- On page 20, Man-yee's dad says her name means **quick** and **fit**. Take turns to think of words with similar meanings for each.

  quick – e.g. *swift, like lightning, high-speed*   fit – e.g. *strong, muscular*